WHAT HAPPENED TO
CHRISTIAN CANADA?

WHAT HAPPENED TO CHRISTIAN CANADA?

Mark A. Noll
University of Notre Dame

REGENT COLLEGE PUBLISHING
Vancouver, Canada

The author and publisher gratefully acknowledge The American
Society of Church History for permission to reprint "What Happened
to Christian Canada?" (*Church History* 75 [June 2006]: 245–273).

Published 2007 by Regent College Publishing
5800 University Boulevard, Vancouver, BC V6T 2E4 Canada
Web: www.regentpublishing.com
E-mail: info@regentpublishing.com

Regent College Publishing is an imprint of the Regent Bookstore
<www.regentbookstore.com>. Views expressed in works published
by Regent College Publishing are those of the author and do not
necessarily represent the official position of Regent College
<www.regent-college.edu>.

Book design by Robert Hand
<www.roberthandcommunications.com>

Library and Archives Canada Cataloguing in Publication

Noll, Mark A., 1946–
What happened to Christian Canada / Mark A. Noll.

ISBN-10: 1–57383–405–X
ISBN-13: 978–1–57383–405–6

1. Christianity—Canada—20th century.
2. Church attendance—Canada.
3. Canada—Church history—20th century.   I. Title

BR570.N54 2007   277.1'0825   C2007-901291-4

CONTENTS

WHAT HAPPENED TO CHRISTIAN CANADA?[1]

I.

By asking "what happened to Christian Canada," I begin with an assumption that there once was a Christian Canada which is now gone. That assumption is intentional. It is intended to highlight not only the dramatic changes that have taken place in Canadian religious life over the last sixty years, but also substantial contrasts between the religious histories of Canada and the United States, which otherwise are so similar in so many

[1] I am grateful to many Canadian scholars and friends for insights that have made this paper possible. At the risk of omitting significant contributions, I would like to thank Phyllis Airhart, Bob Burkinshaw, Nancy Christie, Loraine Coops, Eric Crouse, George Egerton, Michael Gauvreau, Dan Goodwin, Andrew Grenville, Paul Heidebrecht, Bruce Hindmarsh, Harold Jantz, David Jeffrey, Preston Jones, Will Katerberg, Doug Koop, Don Lewis, David Lyon, Ian and Lee Rennie, Bill Reimer, Sam Reimer, Lisa Richmond, John Stackhouse, Brian Stiller, Marguerite Van Die, Marilyn Whitely, and Bill Westfall. My greatest debt of scholarship and friendship is to the late George Rawlyk.

respects.[2] This study explores the question primarily with American observers in mind, for whom the Canadian past is often as much a shadowy mystery as the great expanse of Canadian geography. But I hope Canadians who read this account may benefit from observing how one sympathetic American views their history and also from realizing that the splendid array of marvelous historical studies that have been produced by a splendid array of marvelous Canadian historians have reached at least some appreciative readers in the United States.

A historical snapshot illustrates the contrasts over time with which I am concerned. On September 15, 1959, Georges Vanier was installed as Canada's 19th Governor-General, the Queen's formal representative in her Canadian dominion. Vanier, a much-decorated general, diplomat, and active Roman Catholic began his acceptance speech

---

[2] In attempting what is, in effect, a comparative Canadian-American study, I am following self-consciously in the footsteps of Phyllis D. Airhart, "'As Canadian as Possible Under the Circumstances': Reflections on the Study of Protestantism in North America," in *New Directions in American Religious History*, ed. Harry S. Stout and D. G. Hart (New York: Oxford University Press, 1997), 116-37; William Westfall, "Voices from the Attic: The Canadian Border and the Writing of American Religious History," in *Retelling U.S. Religious History*, ed. Thomas A Tweed (Berkeley: University of California Press, 1997), 181-99; Robert T. Handy, "Protestant Patterns in Canada and the United States," and Paul R. Dekar, "On the Soul of Nations: Religion and Nationality in Canada and the United States," both in *In the Great Tradition*, ed. J. D. Ban and P. R. Dekar (Valley Forge, Penn.: Judson, 1982), 33-51, and 53-72; and especially Robert T. Handy, *A History of the Churches in the United States and Canada* (New York: Oxford University Press, 1977).

like this: "Mr. Prime Minister, my first words are a prayer. May Almighty God in his infinite wisdom and mercy bless the sacred mission which has been entrusted to me by Her Majesty the Queen and help me to fulfill it in all humility. In exchange for his strength, I offer him my weakness. May he give peace to this beloved land of ours and, to those who live in it, the grace of mutual understanding, respect and love."[3]

Fifty-six years later, on September 27, 2005, Michaëlle Jean, became Canada's 27th Governor-General. Jean, a multi-lingual, Haitian-born film-maker and journalist, offered a forward-looking address that stressed, as had Vanier's, the importance of mutual toleration for Canada's social well-being. Otherwise, however, there were no themes in common, for Jean's primary concern was the exaltation of individual liberty; for her, Canadian history "speaks powerfully about the freedom to invent a new world." In this speech there was no mention of the deity.[4]

The contrast with the United States is striking. Vanier's straightforward invocation of God could be likened to the prayer with which Dwight D. Eisenhower began his presidential inaugural in January 1953. And Governor-General Jean's stress on the theme of freedom certainly echoed emphases in the presidential inaugural of George W.

---

[3] Georges P. Vanier, "Inaugural Address," in *Only to Serve: Selections from Addresses of Governor-General Georges P. Vanier*, ed. George Cowley and Michel Vanier (Toronto: University of Toronto Press, 1970), 3.

[4] Michaëlle Jean, "Installation Speech" (Sept. 27, 2005), www. gg.ca/gg/index_e.asp (Nov. 22, 2005).

Bush in January 2005. Yet her sphere of discourse was far removed from both Georges Vanier's 1959 address and the speeches that John Kerry and George Bush made during the 2004 presidential campaign, when talk of God and more general religious matters was noticeably more prominent than it had been in Eisenhower's day.

A second example underscores a similar contrast. Until the recent past Canada's constitutional existence had been enfolded in the common-law traditions of the British parliament before which Americans, with our penchant for thinking that a constitutional democracy requires a written constitution, stand in clueless bemusement. Yet in 1982, after painstaking exertions by Prime Minister Pierre Elliott Trudeau, Canada, with the relieved cooperation of the British parliament, finally took control of its own constitution. Even at that relatively late date public theism remained prominent in Canada's new Charter of Rights and Freedoms. In a complex drafting history, Trudeau first proposed including one off-hand reference to God in the new constitution, which was taken from an earlier Canadian Bill of Rights written during the administration of Conservative leader, John Diefenbaker. That reference was removed because of pressure from members of Trudeau's own Liberal party. But then the issue resurfaced when a broad ecumenical coalition lobbied for formal recognition of Canada's traditional Christian posture. As a result of its pressure, the new Charter was amended to include the following assertion in its preamble: "Canada is founded upon principles that recognize the supremacy of God and the rule of law."[5] The inclusion of such an affirmation in the Charter did not, however, presage a resurgence of traditional Christianity, for under the new Charter, Canadian legislation and jurisprudence have increasingly privileged principles of privacy, multiculturalism, enforced toleration, and public religious neutrality, even when such moves de-christianize public spaces in which religious language was once commonplace.

Education provides another example of significant cultural change. Ontario public schools long included a major place for confessional Christian instruction, even as the province also funded a separate system for its Catholic citizens. This well-established practice, however, came to an end in the recent past. In the words of R. D. Gidney and W. P. J. Millar, "The centrality of Christian doctrine in Ontario's public schools, albeit in a nondenominational Protestant form, was alive and well in the mid-twentieth century; still alive, though less well, as late as the mid-1960s; and, even in the last third of the century, finally ousted only through a prolonged, contested process." But

---

[5] George Egerton, "Trudeau, God, and the Canadian Constitution: Religion, Human Rights, and Government Authority in the Making of the 1982 Constitution," in *Rethinking Church, State, and Modernity: Canada Between Europe and America*, ed. David Lyon and Marguerite Van Die (Toronto: University of Toronto Press, 2000), 99-107. To Egerton's full account, an important supplement on the role played in the Charter debates by evangelical voluntary associations has been provided by Don Page, "From a Private to a Public Religion: The History of the Public Service Christian Fellowship," in *Religion and Public Life in Canada: Historical and Comparative Perspectives*, ed. Marguerite Van Die (Toronto: University of Toronto Press, 2001), 301-02.

the result of this recent change is unmistakable: "In this particular part of the public arena . . . Christianity has not only been disestablished but banished."[6] Inherited religious traditions lasted longer in Quebec and Newfoundland, where virtually all education had been effectively under church supervision until the 1990s. But even in Quebec, which had enjoyed more than two centuries of Catholic educational dominance, and in Newfoundland, which entered the Dominion in 1948 with an explicit guarantee for its government-fund but denominationally-administered school system, the tide of de-christianization has proven irresistible, and education has been secularized.[7]

As once again a mark of strong difference with the United States, the Canadian parliament voted on June 28, 2005, to legalize same-sex marriage throughout all of Canada. That action followed by two years a decision of the Ontario Court of Appeals that the Charter of Rights and Freedom authorized marriage for any two people regardless of gender. When the federal legislation became the law of the land in July 2005, there was minimal public notice, with the only sustained political reservation the Conservative Party's stated desire that Parliament reconsider its vote.[8] Again,

---

[6] R. D. Gidney and W. P. J. Millar, "The Christian Recessional in Ontario's Public Schools," in *Religion and Public Life*, 275, 289.

[7] See Scott Ellis Ferrin, et al., "From Sectarian to Secular Control of Education: The Case of Newfoundland," *Journal of Research on Christian Education* 10 (Fall 2001): 411-30.

[8] For treatment of that Conservative Party opposition, but also of opponents found in the Liberal and New Democratic parties, as well as other pertinent material, see *The Vancouver Sun* for July 23, 2005,

the contrast is striking with the United States, where a judicial action by the Massachusetts Supreme Court similar to the Ontario court's decision—and at about the same time—elicited a storm of national protest and where debate over same-sex marriage became a highly charged factor in many regions during the 2004 elections. In Canada, the redefinition of marriage, which had been unthinkable short decades ago, has been widely, if not universally, accepted.[9] In the United States, the unthinkable has become the contested.

Broad measures of church adherence underscore the magnitude of Canadian religious change over recent decades. As late as 1961, only one-half of one percent of Canadian citizens told Census takers that they were not attached to any religious body. That proportion rose to 4.3% in 1971 and in the latest census from 2001 now stands at 16.2%. Over the same four decades, the proportion of Canadians telling census personnel that they were part of the Catholic church declined slightly from 46% to 43%, while the proportion claiming a connection to the Anglican, Baptist, Presbyterian, and United churches— the four largest Protestant denominations that had long

---

including Peter O'Neil, "Pray," A1, A8; [anon.], "Gay Calgary Couple Altar-Bound," A6; and Doug Ward, "Politics and Prayer" with related articles, E1-E5.

[9] For an academic colloquy dominated by voices opposing this recent change, see Daniel Cere and Douglas Farrow, eds., *Divorcing Marriage: Unveiling the Dangers in Canada's New Social Experiment* (Montreal and Kingston: McGill-Queen's University Press, 2004).

dominated religious life in English-speaking Canada—fell precipitously from 41% to 20%.[10]

Reports of church attendance offer an equally dramatic picture.[11] After World War II, when the Gallup Poll first asked Canadians whether they had been in church or synagogue sometime during the previous seven days, a full 67% of Canadians responded positively. Among all Canadian Catholics, the number was a robust 83% and in Quebec a stratospheric 90%. In the early 1960s, weekly mass attendance in the rapidly growing cities of Montreal and Quebec remained quite high, but some leaders worried openly that in working class neighbors it was down to "only" 50%.[12] By 1990, positive response to the Gallup question had fallen to 23% throughout Canada. Although the foremost Canadian religious demographer, Reginald

---

[10] F. H. Leacy, *Historical Statistics of Canada*, 2nd ed. (Ottawa: Statistics Canada, 1983), Series A164-184; and <www12.statcan.ca/english/census01/products/highlight/Religion> (Dec. 15, 2005).

[11] This paragraph relies on discussion of the Canadian Gallup data on church attendance as found in Reginald W. Bibby, *Fragmented Gods: The Poverty and Potential of Religion in Canada* (Toronto: Irwin, 1987), 16; Reginald W. Bibby, *Unknown Gods: The Ongoing Story of Religion in Canada* (Toronto: Stoddart, 1993), 10; Peter Beyer, "Religious Vitality in Canada: The Complementarity of Religious Market and Secularization Perspectives," *Journal for the Scientific Study of Religion* 36 (1997): 283; and Andrew S. Grenville, "The Awakened and the Spirit-Moved: The Religious Experiences of Canadian Evangelicals in the 1990s," in *Aspects of the Canadian Evangelical Experience*, ed. G. A. Rawlyk (Montreal and Kingston: McGill-Queen's University Press, 1997), 431.

[12] Michael Gauvreau, *The Catholic Origins of Quebec's Quiet Revolution, 1931-1970* (Montreal and Kingston: McGill-Queen's University Press, 2005), 369n15.

Bibby, has recently noted some increase in attendance, his non-Gallup calculations chart a weekly attendance rate for the year 2000 of less than 20%.[13]

Numbers, of course, must be interpreted, but these findings about church identification and church attendance nonetheless indicate a series of shifts in Canadian religion that have not taken place in the United States, or have taken place at a much slower speed. Put generally, in 1950 Canadian church attendance as a proportion of the total population exceeded church attendance in the United States by one-third to one-half, and church attendance in Quebec may have been the highest in the world. Today church attendance in the United States is probably one-half to two-thirds greater than in Canada, and attendance in Quebec is the lowest of any state or province in North America. Over the course of only half a century, these figures represent a dramatic inversion.

This inversion, and the history of the last sixty years that created it, could not have been imagined in the years immediately after the Second World War. At that time, the vigor of Canadian religious practice seemed entirely in keeping with the general trajectory of Canadian history. Not only was Canada more observant in religious practice and more orthodox in religious opinion than the United States, but these comparative results represented only the

---

[13] Reginald W. Bibby, *Restless Gods: The Renaissance of Religion in Canada* (Toronto: Stoddart, 2002), 75-77. For another recent report sensing the possibility of a religious resurgence, see Allan Gregg, "The Christian Comeback," *Saturday Night*, Nov. 2005, pp. 21-22.

latest chapter in a remarkable history of christianization stretching back to the eighteenth century. That history began with the creation in Quebec of a full-orbed, organic Catholic society—grounded in the colonial period on the self-sacrificing labors of several religious orders (both male and female), subsequently renewed by devotional and institutional revivals in the mid-nineteenth century, and then sustained deep into the twentieth century by a hegemonic but still remarkably resilient blend of popular piety and clerical supervision.[14]

In English Canada, the histories were different for the Atlantic provinces, Ontario, the prairies, and the far west, but in each region the end result was similar, and similarly impressive.[15] From precarious beginnings, where

---

[14] For recent overviews, see Gilles Chaussé, "French Canada from the Conquest to 1840," and Roberto Perin, "French-Speaking Canada from 1840," in *A Concise History of Christianity in Canada*, ed. Terrence Murphy and Roberto Perin (Toronto: Oxford University Press, 1996), 56-107, 190-260; a number of helpful articles by Preston Jones, including "Protestants, Catholics, and the Bible in Late-Nineteenth-Century Quebec," *Fides et Historia* 33:2 (Summer/Fall 2001), 31-38; and "Quebec *Indépendentisme* and the Life of Faith," *Journal of Church and State* 43 (Spring 2001): 251-65; Robert Choquette, *Canada's Religions* (Ottawa: University of Ottawa Press, 2004); and especially Jean Hamelin and Nicole Gagnon, *Histoire du catholicisme québécois: Le XXe siècle*, vol. 1: *1898-1940*; and Jean Hamelin, *Histoire du catholicisme québécois: Le XXe siècle*, vol. 2: *De 1940 à nos jours*, both edited by Nive Voisine (Montreal: Boréal, 1984).

[15] For overviews, see George A. Rawlyk, ed., *The Canadian Protestant Experience* (Burlington, Ont.: Welch, 1990); Terrence Murphy, "The English-Speaking Colonies to 1854," and Brian Clarke, "English-Speaking Canada from 1854," in *Concise History of Canada*, 108-89, and 261-360; John Webster Grant, *The Church in the Canadian*

understaffed churches and constantly stretched voluntary agencies performed prodigies, through stressful periods of economic, political, and cultural turmoil—and always confronted by the immensities of uninhabited space—Protestants, along with a strong minority Catholic population, successfully created a Christian civilization in English-speaking Canada that was almost as strong as the French and Catholic counterpart in Quebec. The marks of that civilization included fruitful cooperation between churches and provincial governments in organizing education, social services, and eventually health care; noteworthy syntheses of traditional faith and modern learning that avoided the excesses of both secularization and fundamentalism; deep interpenetration of religious convictions and social values in the outworking of family and community life in many localities;[16] and, not least, steady strengthening of the main denominations, which for most purposes meant

---

Era, 2nd ed. (Burlington, Ont.: Welch, 1988); Choquette, *Canada's Religions*; and especially John Webster Grant, *A Profusion of Spires: Religion in Nineteenth-Century Ontario* (Toronto: University of Toronto Press, 1988).

[16] Important books that document persuasively the deep penetration of Christian values into almost every aspect of local culture (although, of course, not without ambiguity) include Elizabeth Gillan Muir and Marilyn Färdig Whiteley, eds., *Changing Roles of Women Within the Christian Church in Canada* (Toronto: University of Toronto Press, 1995); Lynne Marks, *Revivals and Roller Rinks: Religion, Leisure, and Identity in Late-Nineteenth Small-Town Ontario* (Toronto: University of Toronto Press, 1996); Nancy Christie, ed., *Households of Faith: Family, Gender, and Community in Canada, 1760-1969* (Montreal and Kingston: McGill-Queen's University Press, 2002); and Marguerite Van Die, *Religion, Family, and Community in Victorian Canada: The Colbys*

the Catholics, Anglicans, Presbyterians, Methodists, and Baptists (and from 1925 the United Church of Canada that resulted from the merger of the Methodists and about two-thirds of the Presbyterians.).

The parallel histories of Quebec and the rest of Canada—though never without hypocrisy, patriarchialism, power mongering, partisan conflict, pettimindedness, heavy-handed coercion, inter-denominational strife, and the masquerading of self-interest as piety—nonetheless left Canada at the mid-twentieth century with a much stronger claim as a "Christian nation" than its large neighbor to the south.[17] At least, that is, until the generation after the Second World War when things began to change, and to change in a hurry.

So, what happened? Why did a nation in which until about 1960 almost all measures of Christian faith and practice were stronger than in the United States almost overnight become a nation in which such measures became noticeably weaker? Why, given the sharp historical division between Canada's "two solitudes"—French-speaking, Catholic Quebec and an English-speaking rest of the nation

---

of Carrollcroft (Montreal and Kingston: McGill-Queen's University Press, 2006).

[17] For a general narrative, see Mark A. Noll, "'Christian America' and 'Christian Canada,'" in *The Cambridge History of Christianity*, vol. 8: *World Christianities, c. 1800-c. 1914*, ed. Brian Stanley and Sheridan Gilley (New York: Cambridge University Press, 2006), 359-80; and for a specific argument about the "Christian character" of an earlier Canada, Mark A. Noll, *A History of Christianity in the United States and Canada* (Grand Rapids: Eerdmans, 1992), 545-57.

decisively shaped by a strong Protestant heritage—did both Quebec and the rest of Canada experience just about the same trajectories of de-christianization over just about the same span of time? What can explain the dramatic reversal that Canada's greatest religious historian, John Webster Grant, once put into a single sentence—"Realization that Christendom was dead, even in Canada, dawned with surprising suddenness in the 1960s—at some time during 1965, for many people"—or what an aging priest in Denys Arcand's recent film, *The Barbarian Invasions*, plaintively said about the situation in Quebec: "In 1966 all the churches emptied out in a few weeks. No one can figure out why."[18] The rest of this paper tries to figure out why.

It does so by approaching Canadian history as, in the phrase of David Hackett Fischer, a "web of contingency."[19] The web speaks to the large-scale, tectonic, even deterministic factors in Canadian history. Contingency refers to events, choices, decisions, and actions taken by individuals and groups in that history. By synthesizing web and contingency, I hope it is possible to make some progress in explaining what happened to Christian Canada.

---

[18] Grant, *Church in the Canadian Era*, 216; "Les invasions barbares," written and directed by Denys Arcard (Miramax, 2003).

[19] David Hackett Fischer, "Response to Yerxa, Kersh, Glenn, and Morone," *Historically Speaking*, Sept/Oct 2005, p. 25.

II.

A good beginning point for the web—comparing Canadian and American societies in general—was provided in 1990 by Seymour Margin Lipset's *Continental Divide*, one of the most thoughtful comparative studies of its kind. Lipset's main argument was that Canada "has been and is a more class-aware, elitist, law-abiding, statist, collectivity-oriented, and . . . group-oriented society than the United States."[20] The antistatism, individualism, populism, violence, and egalitarianism that characterize American history have been decidedly less prominent in Canada. Where Canada has stressed the state and community values, the United States has featured the individual and laissez faire. In contrast to the American embrace of individualistic liberalism, Canada has fostered a public attitude stressing communalities, whether "Tory-statist" on the Right or "social democratic" on the Left.

According to Lipset, the reasons for these systematic differences are both geographical and historical. Canada's vast space and sparse population have required a more active government and have placed a premium upon cooperation. Historically, the first move was the most important. In the 1770s Canadians rejected the American Revolution and so were set on a less republican course in both Quebec, where bishops and people remained loyal to Britain despite

---

[20] Seymour Martin Lipset, *Continental Divide: The Values and Institutions of the United States and Canada* (New York: Routledge, 1990), 8.

American diplomacy and invasion, as well as in the Maritimes and Upper Canada, whence many Protestant Loyalists fled after being ejected from their former homes.[21] Then, in the War of 1812, when the outmanned Canadians, with late help from Britain, fended off several American invasions, the result was not only a solidification of Canadian loyalty to Britain, but also a significant reduction of cultural influences from the United States, including ecclesiastical influences.[22]

Canada's own would-be republican revolutions in 1837 and 1838, which (typically) occurred as one effort in Quebec and a different effort in English Canada, fizzled almost completely. The formal disestablishment of Canada's churches took place in the wake of these failed rebellions. Yet in Canada, disestablishment was not a means of dealing with religious pluralism, as in the United States, but of dealing with competing hegemonies. For Quebec, with a fully functioning state-church system, and the rest of Canada, where Anglicans, Presbyterians, and even Methodists had hoped to re-create church-state systems similar to what they

---

[21] See George A. Rawlyk, *Revolution Rejected* (Scarborough, Ont.: Prentice-Hall, 1967); David Mills, *The Idea of Loyalty in Upper Canada, 1784-1850* (Kingston and Montreal: McGill-Queen's University Press, 1988); and Robert M. Calhoon, Timothy M. Barnes, and George A. Rawlyk, eds., *Loyalists and Community in North America* (Westport, CT: Greenwood, 1994).

[22] See Neil Semple, *The Lord's Dominion: The History of Canadian Methodism* (Kingston and Montreal: McGill-Queen's University Press, 1996), 40-49; and J. I. Little, *Borderland Religion: The Emergence of an English-Canadian Identity, 1792-1852* (Toronto: University of Toronto Press, 2004).

had known in Britain, it meant adjustment rather than, as in the United States, all-out denominational competition. In the words of Marguerite Van Die, "A strange paradox happened. In Canada formal disestablishment in reality turned into two informal or shadow establishments, two highly public expressions of religion: Protestantism in English Canada and Roman Catholicism, primarily in Quebec."[23]

The American Civil War frightened Canadians, who for the most part abhorred slavery and yet feared the North's mobilized military might. Reaction to that war was a prime factor hastening creation in 1867 of the Dominion of Canada, which joined Nova Scotia, New Brunswick, Quebec, and Ontario, with Manitoba, British Columbia, and Prince Edward Island coming in shortly thereafter. The Dominion emerged as a free and democratic nation managed by its own responsible government under the imperial surveillance of the British Parliament—in other words, what the thirteen colonies would eventually have become by way of peaceful evolution had not the violent American Revolution intervened. Significantly, however, the founding motto of the new Dominion was simply "peace, order, and good government," which bespoke a more prosaic set of cultural priorities than the Americans' "life, liberty, and the pursuit of happiness." Again, a contrast is

---

[23] Marguerite Van Die, "The End of Christian Canada: Past Perspectives, Present Opportunities for Faith and Public Life" (unpublished paper, delivered at Scarborough United Church, Calgary, September 2002).

important. American independence took place in the 1770s as a reaction against centralized government; with the exception of the Civil War period, Americans refused to accede power to central federal authority until the Great Depression, World War II, and the Civil Rights movement fundamentally altered historic American localism. In Canada, by contrast, Quebec long remained a society that trusted the centralized leadership of the church, and then of business and governmental leaders in league with the church, while "the political culture of Upper Canada," as historian Christopher Adamson has noted, "was statist from its inception."[24] Independence in Canada embraced the centralized authority that independence in America disdained.

In his 1990 volume Lipset cited a number of indicators as evidence for his conclusion about American-Canadian differences: Canada's far lower murder rate, its much fewer number of police per capita, its willingness to tolerate higher taxes, its enforcement of nation-wide gun control, its general contentment with relatively high levels of governmental regulation, and its single-payer health systems that are

---

[24] Christopher Adamson, "Necessary Evil or Necessary Good: Christianity, the State, and Political Culture in the Antebellum United States and Pre-Confederation" (unpublished paper, May 2005), 28, 39. For Adamson's fuller discussion of Canadian-American differences, see "God's Continental Divide: Politics and Religion in Upper Canada and the Northern and Western United States, 1775-1841," *Comparative Studies in Society and History* 36 (July 1994): 417-46.

funded in significant part by the federal government but administered by the provinces.[25]

Of course it is important not to draw too much attention to Canadian-American contrasts. But these contrasts have been significant—first and foremost, the ongoing presence in Canada of two separate societies of relatively equal political weight (French and Catholic, English and Protestant) united in one national polity. Moreover, the emergence in Canada of a free, democratic, and capitalist—but also organic, traditional, statist, and hierarchical—society has led to other systematic differences with the United States, a free, democratic, and capitalist—but also individualistic, innovative, anti-statist, and ideologically egalitarian—society.

In the web, or broad trajectory, of history, Canadians used forces of cohesion to bind a widely scattered people—indeed, two peoples—into a prosperous, well-ordered, and reasonably stable nation-state. Christian faith and practice were critical in building this nation-state. In the United States, active Christianity also contributed materially to the construction of American culture, but it was a religion expressed more in voluntary and individualistic terms, more at home with the operations of a free market, than in Canada where voluntary exertions were always balanced by a reliance upon government, and where free-market initiative was matched by respect for received authority and inherited traditions.

---

[25] Lipset, *Continental Divide*, 92–113.

To move now from the web to contingencies is to take up the events that have precipitated change. Ecclesiastical developments were always intimately related to social and political developments, but for the sake of analysis the wider history is treated first before turning specifically to the church history.

III.

An abbreviated chronology of landmark public events in Canada's recent history might begin with developments in Quebec during the Second World War.[26] In 1940, the province became the last political unit in North America to grant women the right to vote, and in 1943 Quebec for the first time made education compulsory for all children. During the war an ever-growing number of rural Québécois moved to the cities. Shortly thereafter intensifying economic and religious strain produced cracks in the long-standing alliance of social and ecclesiastical elites. In 1949, as an example, key church leaders backed a strike by asbestos workers, and Archbishop Joseph Charbonneau of Montreal was ousted for supporting the strikers.[27]

---

[26] Reliable surveys include Paul-André Linteau, et al., *Histoire du Québec contemporain* (Montreal: Boréal, 1989); and Hamelin, *Histoire du catholicisme québécoise . . . De 1940.*

[27] For recent treatment, see Terence J. Fay, *A History of Canadian Catholics* (Montreal & Kingston: McGill-Queen's University Press, 2002), 249–54.

These events took place under the general political oversight of the Union Nationale party of provincial premier Maurice Duplessis, a crafty pol known as *le Chef* who brokered connections with English business interests and the province's Catholic hierarchy to maintain his conservative government in power from 1944 to 1960. In retrospect, the Duplessis regime must be considered a bottle stop under which great pressure built up to modernize Quebec's economic, political, religious, and cultural strife. The regime achieved stasis, but only by avoiding the province's intensifying push for systematic modernization.

For Canada as a whole, the immediate post-war period mirrored Quebec under Duplessis by communicating an aura of conservative cultural regeneration, but at the expense of addressing profound changes propelled by the Depression, World II, and a post-war boom that included rapidly expanding immigration as well as rapidly expanding wealth. The nation's churches shared fully in the apparent buoyancy. After the War, thousands of lay people joined Sunday School and adult study groups, while from 1945 to 1965 the United Church of Canada by itself constructed over 1,500 churches.[28] In this same period, the charismatic young evangelist, Charles Templeton, who was commissioned by the United Church to conduct a national "Crusade for Christ," offered Canadians their own slightly less aggressive but nearly as effective version of Billy Graham.[29]

---

[28] Grant, *Church in the Canadian Era*, 161.

[29] For consideration of Templeton as an extension of earlier Canadian history, see Kevin Bradley Kee, "Revivalism: The Marketing

In retrospect, however, it is clear that the apparent vigor of the Canadian churches during the 1940s and 1950s owed more to the cohesive nationalism of the war effort and the search for normalcy during a post-war economic expansion than to religious dynamism in the churches themselves. Pierre Berton was not an impartial witness, but when in 1965 he published an indictment of traditional Canadian Christianity, *The Comfortable Pew*, he caught at least something of the placidity that accompanied the post-war boom in church construction: "Christianity has, in the past, always been at its most vigorous when it has been in a state of tension with the society around it. That is no longer the case. . . . In the great issues of our time, the voice of the Church, when it has been heard at all, has been weak, tardy, equivocal, and irrelevant."[30] Berton was certainly correct, perhaps not in the assignment of moral causes, but in anticipating what would soon be acknowledged as the irrelevance of the churches to the pressing issues of Canadian society.

Political changes in the early 1960s marked a beginning of the end for public Canadian life defined by traditional religion. In 1963 the federal Conservative government of John Diefenbaker was defeated by the Liberals under Lester Pearson. Almost immediately the new Liberal government

---

of Protestant Religion in English-speaking Canada, with Particular Reference to Southern Ontario, 1884-1957" (Ph.D. diss., Queen's University, 1999).

[30] Pierre Berton, *The Comfortable Pew* (Philadelphia: J. B. Lippincott, 1965), 16.

agreed to let the United States install nuclear weapons in the Canadian North. This action, in turn, precipitated a notable book from George Parkin Grant, a philosopher and public intellectual whose singular stance combined a great deal of Anglican traditionalism with much social liberalism and moral conservatism. His book, *Lament for a Nation*, was a widely noticed critique of economic and ethical individualism, the Cold War, and American democracy as corrosive solvents of Canada's historic Christian cultures, but it did not turn the tide.[31]

Meanwhile in Quebec, the reign of Duplessis's Union Nationale came to an end in 1960 with the triumph of the provincial Liberal Party in which an active cadre of reforming Catholic intellectuals, including Pierre Elliot Trudeau, eagerly pushed for a new order. In that same year, Quebec's labor unions, which had always been Catholic organizations, broke their tie with the church.

What followed was Quebec's "revolution tranquille," which was in fact anything but "quiet." In 1964 a provincial Ministry of Education was created; for the first time in Quebec's history the Catholic church was not in control of the province's schools. Criticisms of Catholic institutions of a sort once rarely heard were now commonplace. Voices

---

[31] George Parkin Grant, *Lament for a Nation: The Defeat of Canadian Nationalism* (Toronto: McClelland and Stewart, 1965). On the book's impact, see William Christian, *George Grant: A Biography* (Toronto: University of Toronto Press, 1994), 240-55.

calling for greater autonomy in Quebec over against the rest of Canada began to speak as much about linguistic and economic distinctives as about Quebec's Catholic heritage. Vocations to the priesthood and the religious orders plummeted. In the summer of 1967 Charles De Gaulle visited from France and proclaimed to a huge outdoor rally in Montreal, "Vive le Québec libre!" His dramatic words added fuel to a fire of secular nationalism that was already burning brightly. In the late 1960s, radicals of the Front de Liberátion du Quebec trumpeted Marx, robbed banks, and assassinated a provincial minister. The attempt at armed revolution did not succeed, but the terrorist actions, along with the draconian counter-measures of the national Liberal government, now led by Pierre Elliot Trudeau, raised the political temperature considerably. Almost overnight, it seemed, Quebec's stable synthesis of Catholic, French, rural, conservative, isolationist, and pre-capitalist values had disappeared.

Meanwhile, in the rest of Canada, historic markers of Christian civilization seemed to give way almost as rapidly, if with slightly less revolutionary impact. A recent study by Gary Miedema has shown how at signal events in 1967—celebrations of Canada's centennial and Expo 67 at Montreal's World Exposition—public symbols and rhetoric moved away from particulars of Canada's religious and ethnic history toward a vision of universal multicultural toleration. On these well-publicized occasions, public spokespeople looked to the latter rather than the former to "foster unity, stability, and a common vision in a country perpetually challenged by division, political instability, and multiple and conflicting dreams for the future."[32]

In 1969, Trudeau's Liberal government engineered a declaration that made all of Canada officially bilingual. To Reginald Bibby, this was a key event in the process whereby an ideology of pluralism replaced the traditional Christian ideologies of both French and English Canada. In his view this declaration revealed that, "since the 1960s, Canada has been encouraging the freedom of groups and individuals without simultaneously laying down cultural expectations." According to Bibby, "colorful collages of mosaics have been forming throughout Canadian life. Our expectation has been that fragments of the mosaic will somehow add up to a healthy and cohesive society. It is not at all clear why we should expect such an outcome."[33]

Then in 1971 the government began to promote multiculturalism as a national policy. This decision led to government agencies and funds explicitly devoted to promoting the self-consciousness of ethnic minorities. Equal access and mutual respect were assuming the public place that had once been occupied by recognition of the deity. In 1980 Quebec separatists, who had been partly energized by elements of Trudeau's political liberalism but who then

---

[32] I am quoting Gary R. Miedema, "For Canada's Sake: The Re-visioning of Canada and the Re-structuring of Public Religion in the 1960s" (Ph.D. diss., Queen's University, 2000), 27; but see also the book from this dissertation, *For Canada's Sake: Public Religion, Centennial Celebrations, and the Re-making of Canada in the 1960s* (Kingston and Montreal: McGill-Queen's University Press, 2005).

[33] Bibby, *Mosaic Madness* (Toronto: Stoddart, 1990), 10.

felt betrayed by his staunch defense of a unified Canada, succeeded in bringing a separation resolution to vote in that province. It failed, but narrowly.

The repatriation of the Constitution and the new Charter of Rights and Freedom followed in 1982, after which perpetual political crisis became the order of the day. The most consequential long-term effect of the new Charter was to push Canadian jurisprudence into an increasingly American pattern where activistic judges become the promoters of social change.[34] What Seymour Martin Lipset noted and predicted in 1990 has in fact come to pass: "The Charter of Rights . . . probably goes further toward taking the country in an American direction than any other enacted structural change, including the Canada-U.S. Free Trade Agreement. The Charter's stress on due process and individual rights, although less stringent than that of the U.S. Bill of Rights, should increase individualism and litigiousness north of the border."[35]

The most immediate results of repatriation, however, were political rather than judicial. Prime Minister Trudeau, although himself from Quebec, had more success convincing the rest of Canada that the new constitution was a good thing than he did with Quebec, which, nervous about protecting

---

[34] For an argumentative, but still informative, discussion of judicial changes since 1982, see Robert Ivan Martin, *The Most Dangerous Branch: How the Supreme Court of Canada Has Undermined Our Law and Our Democracy* (Montreal and Kingston: McGill-Queen's University Press, 2003).

[35] Lipset, *Continental Divide*, 116.

its hereditary prerogatives, refused to ratify the document. Under Brian Mulroney, the Progressive Conservative who became prime minister in 1984, provincial leaders hammered out an agreement in 1987 at a government retreat house on Quebec's Meech Lake that was designed to secure Quebec's assent to the Constitution. This Meech Lake Accord designated Quebec as a "distinct society" and expanded the control it could exercise over its own affairs. But for a mixture of reasons—including dissatisfaction about special privileges offered to Quebec, a desire by other provinces also to gain greater autonomy from Ottawa, and Native American contentions for ethnic rights—the Meech Lake Accord failed to secure the approval of all provinces by the stipulated date for its ratification, June 1990.

The failure of the Meech Lake Accord rekindled efforts by Quebec separatists to leave the Dominion, which led in 1995 to another provincial plebiscite on separation. This vote again failed, but by the narrowest of margins. Significantly, as in the earlier plebiscite, French-speaking Québécois who were active in their Catholic parishes were more likely to vote to remain with Canada than those who were not.[36] For them, practicing a historical religion seems to have provided a reason for cherishing the historical Canada.

Mostly as a result of agitation over Quebec's push for independence, along with western resistance at rule from the center, Canada's traditional political alignments have been almost completely overturned. For more than a century from

---

[36] Andrew Grenville and Angus Reid, "Catholicism and Voting No," *ChristianWeek*, Jan. 30, 1996, p. 7.

the founding in 1867, Liberal and Progressive Conservatives had alternated governments with, from the 1930s, a significant minority contribution from two other parties that arose as social protest movements on the prairies: the New Democratic Party representing democratic socialists of the Left and Social Credit representing populists who combined moral conservativism and trust in large-scale government. Where the Liberals and Progressive Conservatives always cultivated their ties to leaders of Canada's main churches, the New Democrats and Social Credit arose quite directly from the actions of Christian clergymen.[37]

Over the last two decades this once stable configuration has given way. The Progressive Conservative party collapsed when it lost the confidence of its constituencies in Quebec and the Canadian West. As the national debate over Quebec separatism heated up, a new federal party, the Bloc Québécois, has arisen to dominate federal elections in that province. In the West appeared a Reform Party that appealed for less deference to Ontario and Quebec and that advocated a social and cultural agenda similar to moderate Democrats and moderate Republicans in the United States. Most recently the Reform Party has merged with the

---

[37] On the Baptist socialist, Tommy Douglas, who founded the Cooperative Commonwealth Confederation, which eventually became the New Democratic Party, see Doris French Shackleton, *Tommy Douglas* (Toronto: McClelland and Stewart, 1975); and on William Aberhart, the radio Bible teacher and independent fundamentalist pastor who helped found the Social Credit party and long served as Alberta's premier, see David R. Elliott and Iris Miller, *Bible Bill: A Biography of William Aberhart* (Edmonton: Reidmore, 1987).

tattered remnants of the old Progressive Conservatives to form a new Conservative Party, which in the election of January 2006 finally succeeded in dislodging the Liberals from their long hold on federal leadership.

This tangled political history is important for religion since the older parties had enjoyed familiar affinities with Canada's main denominations in a way that has almost completely vanished.[38] Questions of regional power now compete with questions of economic influence as the drivers of Canadian political life. Ongoing debate over the effects of the North America Free Trade Agreement, which was approved in 1992; ongoing disagreement over the disposition of wealth generated by Alberta's oil, Quebec's hydro-electricity, and Ontario's manufacturing and service industries; ongoing arguments over how to regulate the flood of American cultural products and business investment; ongoing resentment from the Atlantic and prairie provinces about lack of attention from Ottawa—these issues have joined the everlasting constitutional contentions to dominate the political landscape. In the late 1980s, John Webster Grant perceptively summarized the religious effect of these preoccupations: "The unofficial establishment of

---

[38] See, for example, an excellent recent survey in the *Economist* where religion is not mentioned even once, which would have been inconceivable in any broad study of Canadian political and economic life in earlier periods; Peter David, "Peace, Order, and Rocky Government," *Economist*, Dec. 3, 2005, pp. 1-16 of special section. For specific commentary on the absence of religion from a similar earlier survey in *Maclean's* magazine, see Harold Jantz, "Some Thoughts on the Healing of a Nation," *ChristianWeek*, July 16, 1991, p. 6.

Christianity in Canada, already in 1967 more shadow than substance, is in 1987 little more than a memory." Grant went on to say that religion, long an overarching reality in Canada, had become only "a set of personal wants analogous to other wants."[39]

From 1980 onwards economic and political preoccupations have almost completely eclipsed all other contenders, including religion, in dominating Canadian public space. Put more exactly, historic Canadian tensions, like the struggle between Quebec and the rest of Canada, which once were expressed in religious terms, have now come to be expressed almost entirely in terms of political and economic power.

IV.

For the purposes of analysis, it is critical to realize that Canada's complicated recent history of economic debate and political realignment has also been its history of de-christianization. The social cohesion that the churches once provided is now offered by political and economic loyalties or by ideologies of toleration, personal growth, and multiculturalism. In the changes of recent decades, however, the churches have acted as well as been acted upon. These actions played out differently for Catholics, the United Church, Anglicans, and Canada's sectarian and evangelical churches, but no actions were more important than those of

---

[39] Grant, *Church in the Canadian Era*, 240, 241.

the Catholics in Quebec and the United Church throughout all of Canada.

From the 1930s on, an eerie and even ironic confluence of similar forces affected these two great churches. In both cases an active cadre of intelligent and dedicated leaders promoted the same sort of reformist agenda over against the churches' inherited traditions. The confluence is eerie because the Protestant and Roman Catholic stories were worked out in very different arenas with very little contact between the two. The confluence has been immensely significant because the Roman Catholic Church and the United Church were the most important institutional bearers of Canada's traditional Christian culture.

Roman Catholicism in Quebec from the 1930s

For the much debated subject of Quebec's revolutionary transformation in the 1960s and afterwards, it is important to acknowledge the complexities at work. Certainly the petrified state of the institutional church and the hierarchy's unsuccessful efforts at adjusting to new circumstances played a part.[40] Also significant were efforts to modernize Quebec's traditional rural economy and to wrest control of Quebec's economic future from Anglo and Protestant business

---

[40] See especially Gregory Baum, "Catholicism and Secularization in Quebec," in his *The Church in Quebec* (Ottawa: Novalis, 1991), 15-48.

elites.[41] The growing scale of governmental authority, both locally and federally, were doubtless also important.[42] And the role of a new generation of intellectuals with an eye for power certainly came into play.[43] But for dramatic changes in religious life it is most important to examine changes within religious life itself, for which purpose a persuasive set of arguments advanced recently by Michael Gauvreau of McMaster University are especially helpful.[44]

As a useful point of reference it is well to remember that during the century before 1960 the Catholic church maintained a steady average of one priest for every 500-700 Quebec parishioners, one of the lowest ratios in the Catholic world.[45] As late as 1961, there were almost 43,000

----

[41] See especially Michael D. Behiels, *Prelude to Quebec's Quiet Revolution: Liberalism versus Neo-Nationalism, 1945-1960* (Montreal and Kingston: McGill-Queen's University Press, 1985).

[42] See Daniel Latouche, "La vrai nature de . . . la Revolution tranquille," *Candian Journal of Political Science/Revue canadienne de science politique* 7 (Sept. 1974): 525-36.

[43] See especially Léon Dion, "Une conscience critique de l'ancien régime: La quéte de la modernité," in his *Québec, 1945-2000*, vol. 2: *Les intellectuals et le temps de Duplessis* (Sainte-Foy, Quebec: Les Presses de l'Université Laval, 1993), 139-412.

[44] See Michael Gauvreau, "From Rechristianization to Contestation: Catholic Values and Quebec Society, 1931-1970," *Church History* 69 (Dec. 2000): 803-33; "The Emergence of Personalist Feminism: Catholicism and the Marriage-Preparation Movement in Quebec, 1940-1966," in *Households of Faith*, 319-47; and *The Catholic Origins of Quebec's Quiet Revolution* (note 12 above).

[45] Hamelin and Gagnon, *Histoire du catholicisme québécois . . . 1898-1940*, 124.

women in religious orders (about three-fifths educators), or one for about every 115 Quebec Catholics.[46]

Yet by the 1930s there also existed in the church new voices to challenge the hierarchy's traditional, clergy-directed conceptions of piety and the province's conservative and capitalist economic conventions. These new voices, heavily influenced by reformist Catholicism in France, promoted personalist theology for the mind and Catholic Action for society.[47] To these reformers, state intervention and economic planning marked out the paths to social justice, while piety was best re-defined as service to and in the world. Led by figures like Father Joseph-Papin Archambault, François Hertel, the brothers Alex and Gérard Pelletier, and eventually a corps of young lawyers including Pierre Eliot Trudeau, these revisionist Catholics sought to define a faith that could solve the problems of the Depression and energize Quebec for the post-war world. Critically, these early advocates of Catholic Action sought religious renewal, especially for women and the working classes, by promoting a clean break with earlier forms of Quebec's Catholic social order, which they regarded as hopelessly primitive. The result was a religious perspective that looked to social collectivism and theological innovation as reliable guides for modernization.

---

[46] Nicole Laurin, Danielle Juteau, and Lorraine Duchesne, *À la recherche d'un monde oublié: Les communautés réligieuses de femmes au Québec de 1900 à 1970* (Montreal: LeJour, 1991), 55.

[47] The content of that personalism is spelled out in Gauvreau, "From Rechristianization to Contestation."

Important shifts in attitudes toward marriage and the family were central for this new form of peoples and reformist Catholicism. Through various youth organizations sponsored by Catholic Action, particularly the Service de Preparation au Mariage (SPM), articulate Catholic laywomen and laymen argued that a drastic reform was needed for the intergenerational, patriarchal, and emotionally impoverished family of the past in order to pursue a new "ideal of marriage . . . based upon personal choice, love, and sexual fulfillment."[48] Although this program operated self-consciously within the church, its advocacy of what Gauvreau calls "personalist feminism" shifted Catholic attitudes away from clerically defined traditions toward new possibilities of personal freedom, especially for women. The importance of such new instruction for what came later is that the SPM's activity encouraged women to seek sexual satisfaction in marriage, to control the timing and number of their children, and even (at least before the promulgation of *Humanae Vitae* in 1968) to explore the possibility of using birth control pills to regulate reproduction. The larger issue is not that the SPM was actively subverting the loyalty of the Québécois to Roman Catholicism, but rather that within the church itself there were clear signals of new cultural values even at the height of the Duplessis era of apparent conformity to the traditional norms of Catholic corporatist society.

---

[48] Gauvreau, "Emergence of Personalist Feminism," 327.

The latent power of the new perspective was heightened by the fact that traditionalist elements in Quebec's Roman Catholicism were moribund. Leaders of the older Catholicism seemed to survive in good shape, and in control of society, through the long tenure of Premier Duplessis. But they had none of the drive of the younger laymen and laywomen who were applying currents of Catholic personalism from Europe with unusual effect. In retrospect, it is evident that in their eager cooperation with the Duplessis regime, Quebec's clerical, traditional Catholics had traded their religious birthright for a pottage of corrupt political patronage. From this angle, traditional Catholics did not so much lose Quebec as give it away.

Then in the late 1940s and 1950s, a better educated, more cosmopolitan core of leaders arose to direct the public course of Catholic Action. These later reformers also sought Catholic renewal, but as the project of a new intelligentsia that turned its scorn not only against the rural conservatism of traditional Quebec society, but also the working class renewal movements of earlier Catholic Action. These new intellectuals, whose most visible representative eventually became Trudeau, also promoted the need for a rupture with the past, but went even further than the early advocates of Catholic Action by arguing that public (even secular) institutions could achieve the social renewal they desired.

The vision of these elites included an even stronger sense of the need for a break with the past; a total critique of the conservative Duplessis-clerical alliance; a completely new vision of what Catholic public order should look like; and a belief that these comprehensive reforms needed to be carried out by professional elites controlling the machinery of state instead of clerical elites or lay working class Catholics or English business magnates.

In the event, both phases of Catholic Action were successful in convincing Quebec of the need for a rupture with older forms of Catholicism, but they were not successful in getting the citizens of Quebec to embrace their version of a reformed, modern Catholicism. Rather, most Quebec citizens, when they gave up the older form of traditional Catholicism, turned to the a- or anti-Catholic forms of nationalism, state rule, and linguistic sovereignty promoted by more secular or even radical forces.

The irony was that while the new perspective was successful at winning the mind of the church in the decades after the Depression, it left the church in the 1960s with almost nothing specifically Christian to say to the radically transformed society of this latter era. Here is how Michael Gauvreau puts it: "In the process of articulating this youthful, new Catholicism, its lay promoters originated the central cultural concept undergirding the Quiet Revolution: that a fundamental rupture divided the present from the past, a gulf that necessitated an entirely new framework of personal, familial, and social identities."[49] In the admirably succinct summary of historian Preston Jones: "French Canadian nationalism as a cultural disposition rooted in Quebec's Catholic history was transformed into Quebecois

---

[49] Gauvreau, *Catholic Origins*, 354.

separatism as a secular faith founded upon an aspiration for political salvation from the influences of the English."[50] In a word, the personalism of Social Catholicism had captured, but it could not feed, the soul of Quebec.

The United Church of Canada

The story of the United Church points to a strikingly similar conclusion, though the plot unfolds against strikingly different terrain.[51] Throughout the nineteenth century, the Presbyterians and Methodists, along with Baptists in the Maritimes and Anglicans throughout Canada, had provided the Protestant energy that built an English-speaking Christian nation. Both Presbyterians, with leaders like Principal George Monro Grant of Queen's University, and Methodists, with leaders like Nathanael Burwash of Victoria College in Toronto, had featured a well-balanced liberal evangelicalism which was almost as committed to a supernatural Gospel as their American evangelical contemporaries and almost as devoted to the power of a social Gospel as their mainline American contemporaries.[52] In addition, both Methodists and Presbyterians had

---

[50] Jones, "Quebec *Indépendentisme*," 252.

[51] For background, I am drawing on Grant, *Church in the Canadian Era*, 124-28, 171-76, 186-87.

[52] See Marguerite Van Die, *An Evangelical Mind: Nathanael Burwash and the Methodist Tradition in Canada, 1839-1918* (Montreal and Kingston: McGill-Queen's University Press, 1989); D. B. Mack, "George Monro Grant: Evangelical Prophet" (Ph.D. diss., Queen's University, 1992); and more generally Michael Gauvreau, *The Evangelical Century: College and Creed in English Canada from the Great Revival*

articulated a powerful message of Christian social order that, again by comparison with main Protestant bodies in the United States, relied less on world-despising individualism and practiced more integration of public and private moral responsibility.[53]

Then in 1925, after more than twenty years of negotiations, the Methodists and a majority of the Presbyterians agreed to merge into the United Church of Canada.[54] From its origins, the new United Church saw itself as distinctly a national church, even *the* national church, that could provide the informal establishment that Canada needed to continue as a moral, God-honoring, and socially compassionate country. In the words of a leading historian of Canadian Methodism, Neil Semple, "The support for church union was heavily bound up with the optimistic vision for Canada itself. . . . If Canada's destiny was to have a spiritual and moral base, a patriotic national church must instill a common set of Christian principles, help preserve national and social stability, guide the country's conscience, and make Canada a legitimate model for the entire world."[55]

---

to the Great Depression (Montreal and Kingston: McGill-Queen's University Press, 1991).

[53] See especially Phyllis D. Airhart, "Ordering a New Nation and Reordering Protestantism, 1867-1914," in *The Canadian Protestant Experience*, 98-138.

[54] The most penetrating account remains N. Keith Clifford, *The Resistance to Church Union in Canada, 1904-1939* (Vancouver: University of British Columbia Press, 1985).

[55] Semple, *The Lord's Dominion*, 427.

When, however, Methodists and the majority of Presbyterians finalized Church Union, they were denominations in transition. In both groups a newer concern for social transformation as an end in itself and a wariness of former evangelical enthusiasm was beginning to compete against the older liberal evangelicalism.[56] That competition between these two forces did in fact continue in the United Church at large until the final victory in the 1960s of social collectivism and theological modernism. But the mind of the United Church was captured by these newer forces well before the church itself.

Nancy Christie has recently provided a provocative interpretation of how those changes occurred, by specific reference to the United Church's official stance on marriage, sexuality, and the family.[57] Her contention is that

---

[56] On the denominational heritages that were being transformed, see Phyllis D. Airhart, *Serving the Present Age: Revivalism, Progressivism, and the Methodist Tradition in Canada* (Kingston and Montreal: McGill-Queen's University Press, 1992); and John S. Moir, *Early Presbyterianism in Canada*, ed. Paul Laverdure (Gravelbourg, Sask.: Laverdure, 2003). Contrasting views on what those transformations signified are ably presented in David B. Marshall, *Secularizing the Faith: Canadian Protestant Clergy and the Crisis of Belief, 1850-1940* (Toronto: University of Toronto Press, 1992); and Nancy Christie and Michael Gauvreau, *A Full-Orbed Christianity: The Protestant Churches and Social Welfare in Canada, 1900-1940* (Kingston and Montreal: McGill-Queen's University Press, 1996). To Marshall, they were signs of triumphant secularism; to Christie and Gauvreau, they represented potentially productive adaptations.

[57] Nancy Christie, "Sacred Sex: The United Church and the Privatization of the Family in Post-War Canada," in *Households of Faith*, 348-76. Her findings echo, at least in part, the arguments by

United Church leaders by the 1940s felt they were being marginalized by the expanding reach of the new Canadian welfare state, especially as represented by the Family Allowances Act of 1944. In response, church leaders turned to a neo-orthodox theology that, in effect, repudiated Canada's long tradition of an active social gospel. At the same time, they also redefined the place of the family as private rather than public, as existing for the sexual and personal satisfaction of spouses instead of for the moral well-being of Canadian society, and as designed less for triumph over sin than as an arena for self-realization. By 1960, the orthodox aspects of neo-orthodox theology were wearing away, and the commitment to personal self-fulfillment was becoming ever stronger. The result, according to Christie, was, first, that the United Church's efforts to contain the expansion of the federal government "had peculiarly liberal results . . . in establishing the cultural preconditions for modern sexual mores"; and, second, that "by 1966, after two hundred years of forming the core of Methodist and Presbyterian theology, evangelicalism in mainline Protestantism foundered upon the rock of modern gender identities and human sexuality."[58]

The latent power of this new theology of modernism and ethics of privatized selfhood was heightened by the fact that traditionally evangelical elements in the United Church

---

Callum Brown on the role of gender and women's issues in the rapid de-christianization of post-war Britain; see Brown, *The Death of Christian Britain* (New York: Routledge, 2001).

[58] Ibid., 349, 366.

could never quite establish an effective public presence, neither in the decades immediately after church union, nor in the century's middle decades of theology drift, nor in the recent period as a counter to liberalizing elements in the denomination.[59] The irony of the situation was that while a modernistic social gospel succeeded in winning the mind of the United Church, that victory left the United Church with little to offer by way of specific Christian content in the radically transformed conditions of the 1960s, when Canadian governments acted far more effectively than the churches in guaranteeing personal welfare.

In sum, the ability of what had once been a socially responsible, moderately intellectual, Arminian evangelical Methodism and a socially responsible, reasonably comprehensive, Calvinistic Presbyterianism to make any kind of a sharp Christian impact on Canadian thought, society, politics, or spirituality was fatally compromised by what Barry Mack has very precisely labeled "the tragic failure of Church Union."[60]

The Disengagement of the Anglican Church of Canada

The story of Canadian Anglicanism, which had been the socially dominant church of English Canada for most of

---

[59] See David Plaxton, "'We Will Evangelize with a Whole Gospel or None': Evangelicalism and the United Church of Canada," in *Aspects of the Canadian Evangelical Experience*, 106-22.

[60] Barry Mack, "From Preaching to Propaganda to Marginalization: The Lost Centre of Twentieth-Century Presbyterianism," in *Aspects of the Canadian Evangelical Experience*, 138.

the nineteenth century, does not exactly parallel the story of either Quebec Catholicism or the United Church.[61] Rather, the ability of Anglicans to act effectively in Canada gradually receded as Canadian society moved further and further from the deferential assumptions of the colonial period when Anglicanism acted as a church establishment—sometimes formal, often informal—in guiding English Canada's elite, especially in Ontario.

In a forceful series of books and articles, William Westfall has shown how Canadian Anglicans attempted to exert cultural authority through university education, through urban architecture, and through influence on social elites, but all with diminishing returns.[62] As the principle of informal establishment faded along with the assumptions of Christendom, Canadian Anglicans were left at sea. Robertson Davies, noted novelist, journalist, playwright, and the most visible Anglican layman of the twentieth century, was a good case in point, since his own theology was as heterodox as his writing was captivating, and his

---

[61] For general treatments, see Curtis Fahey, *In His Name: The Anglican Experience in Upper Canada, 1791-1854* (Ottawa: Carleton University Press, 1991); and William H. Katerberg, *Modernity and the Dilemma of North American Anglican Identities, 1880-1950* (Kingston and Montreal: McGill-Queen's University Press, 2001).

[62] William Westfall, *Two Worlds: The Protestant Culture of Nineteenth-Century Ontario* (Montreal and Kingston: McGill-Queen's University Press, 1989); *The Founding Moment: Church, Society, and the Construction of Trinity College* (Montreal and Kingston: McGill-Queen's University Press, 2002); and "Constructing Public Religions at Private Sites: The Anglican Church in the Shadow of Disestablishment," in *Religion and Public Life*, 23-49.

appeal for "numinosity" as the soul of Canadian religion was as vague as his novels were compellingly concrete.[63] More recently, efforts by Anglicans to preserve a measure of social influence have been set back by extensive court battles arising from earlier abuses of First Nation's children in residential schools and by corrosive internal debates on matters of sexuality and doctrine.[64] The struggle to define a meaningful Anglican presence for a denomination now marked by wide doctrinal pluralism leaves little energy for the magisterial guidance the denomination once provided for at least some ranks of Canadian society.

Canada's Sectarian and Evangelical Churches

By the 1940s, representatives of Canada's "other churches" were beginning to manifest considerable strength. These included immigrant bodies like the Mennonites, the Dutch Reformed, the Lutherans, the various Orthodox churches, and the Greek Catholics. More numerously, they were represented by a host of conservative evangelical bodies like the Christian and Missionary Alliance, the Plymouth Brethren, the Salvation Army, several Pentecostal denominations, and still others who were able to establish

---

[63] On "numinosity," see Robertson Davies, "Keeping Faith," *Saturday Night* 102 (Jan. 1987): 187-192 (esp. 190).

[64] For background, see J. R. Miller, "The State, the Church, and Indian Residential Schools in Canada," in *Religion and Public Life*, 109-29; and Alan Hayes, *Anglicans in Canada: Controversies and Identity in Historical Perspective* (Urbana: University of Illinois Press, 2004).

flourishing works in particular locales.[65] More recently, country-wide associations like the Evangelical Fellowship of Canada have begun the process of drawing locally vital evangelical bodies into some form of national cohesion.[66]

Yet although such efforts have become increasingly important, they have not affected the broader society as Catholics and the older Protestants had once done. For various reasons—ethnicity, language, a passivity-inducing Holiness theology, or a stultifying fixation on biblical prophecy—these "other" Christians have often been content to remain in self-contained social, intellectual, and cultural ghettoes.

Brian Stiller is only one among many who have come to such conclusions, but from his former position as head of the Evangelical Fellowship of Canada and now as president of Ontario's Tyndale University College, one of the nation's

---

[65] For an outstanding case study of one such local situation, see D. Bruce Hindmarsh, "The Winnipeg Fundamentalist Network, 1910-1940: The Roots of Transdenominational Evangelicalism in Manitoba and Saskatchewan," *Aspects of the Canadian Evangelical Experience,* 303-19.

[66] See Page, "From a Private to a Public Religion"; Kevin Quast and John Vissers, eds., *Studies in Canadian Evangelical Renewal: Essays in Honour of Ian S. Rennie* (Markham, Ont.: Faith Today, 1996); and several works by John G. Stackhouse, Jr., including "Bearing Witness: Christian Groups Engage Canadian Politics since the 1960s," in *Rethinking Church, State, and Modernity,* 113-28; "'Who Whom?' Evangelism and Canadian Society," in *Aspects of the Canadian Evangelical Experience,* 55-70; "The Historiography of Canadian Evangelicalism: A Time to Reflect," *Church History* 64 (Dec. 1995): 627-34; and *Canadian Evangelicalism in the Twentieth Century* (Toronto: University of Toronto Press, 1993).

few confessionally religious colleges, his analysis deserves special attention: "While maintaining their growth patterns and surprising many by their ability to attract Baby Boomers, [evangelical Protestants'] lack of involvement in the cultural mainstream has served to keep them from making a great deal of difference in the culture. Trapped for much of this century in a sectarian mode—a withdrawal from mainstream considerations and activities—evangelicals have only recently become concerned with what is going on in the public sphere. But, in terms of cultural influence, they are all very much outsiders."[67]

From one angle, these Canadian sectarians, evangelicals, Pentecostals, and ethnic denominationalists are flourishing because they seem to have followed an American pattern of self-protecting atomism—by attending to local situations and avoiding the national Big Picture, they have done quite well. But from another angle, the American comparison reveals dissimilarities.[68] The relatively small size and modest means of the sectarian cohort in Canada, compared to the much larger and much wealthier cohort in the United States,

---

[67] Brian Stiller, *From the Tower of Babel to Parliament Hill: How to Be a Christian in Canada Today* (Toronto: HarperCollins, 1997), 19-20.

[68] For the most extensive cross-border comparisons of evangelicals, and one of the best cross-border studies of any kind, see Sam Reimer, *Evangelicals and the Continental Divide: The Conservative Protestant Subculture in Canada and the United States* (Montreal and Kingston: McGill-Queen's University Press, 2003).

constitutes a major difference. But so does the fact that voluntaristic sectarians flourish in the United States at least in part because their loose, traditionless, entrepreneurial style fits well with the United States' historically looser, less traditional, more republican, and more entrepreneurial culture, whereas north of the border no form of sectarianism or voluntarism has ever exerted a major public influence in Canada's more corporate, conformist, cooperative, and monarchical culture.

The Second Vatican Council

As a final element in Canada's recent ecclesiastical history, it is important to highlight the significance of the Second Vatican Council. The role of the Council was obviously important for Canada's Catholics, but may have been almost as significant for its Protestants. In Quebec, but also for Canadian Catholics in general, the Council was destabilizing because it rapidly altered the liturgy, the language, the music, the tone, the disciplines, and the calendrical observances that for a great part of the faithful had simply constituted the meaning of the faith. In this sense, Canada resembled Western European Catholicism, which was also disconcerted by the Council, rather than Eastern European, African, and Asian Catholicism, which was energized by its work.

Certainly it was critically important that for Quebec the Second Vatican Council took place at exactly the same time as the transition from the Duplessis regime to the new Liberal government. The combination of rapid change in the church and rapid change in politics goes far toward explaining what Gregory Baum has called "an unexpected secularization of personal consciousness."[69]

But if the specifically Canadian effect of the Second Vatican Council was to confuse what Christianity meant for Roman Catholics, the Council may have done the same for Protestants. A wealth of scholarship has documented in varying ways how important a negative image of the Catholic church had always been for English-speaking Protestants, and with growing force from the eighteenth century onward.[70] To be an active Protestant in many parts of the world was of course to believe and practice certain Protestant verities. But it was also to be self-consciously and very seriously anti-Roman Catholic. While Canada's national political leaders from Wilfred Laurier, the first Catholic premier who took office in 1896, knew how to finesse Catholic-Protestant suspicion in public life, that suspicion remained an important aspect of Protestant identity. The point to be made for the 1960s is that, precisely when both Protestants and Roman Catholics were undergoing increasing strain for other reasons, the Second Vatican Council exerted a direct effect on Canada's Roman Catholics, but also an indirect effect on Canada's Protestants.

---

[69] Gregory Baum, "Catholicism and Secularization in Quebec," in *Rethinking Church, State, and Modernity*, 164.

[70] Outstanding examples include John Wolffe, *The Protestant Crusade in Britain, 1829-1860* (New York: Oxford University Press, 1991); and Linda Colley, *Britons: Forging the Nation, 1707-1839* (New Haven: Yale University Press, 1992).

At virtually a stroke, the Council and then the rapid decline of Christian practice greatly reduced Protestant reasons to fear a monolithic, archly traditional, ultramontane Roman Catholicism. Since that fear had long been a prop for serious Protestant adherence in Canada, the Canadian Roman Catholic reaction to the Second Vatican Council may have done almost as much damage to Canadian Protestants as it did to Canadian Roman Catholics.

Reactions to the Second Vatican Council resemble the other signal events of Canada's recent history. No one event by itself can explain the speed and magnitude of ecclesiastical change. But without attention to specific developments within the churches, there is no satisfying general account of Canada's recent history.

V.

So, what happened to Christian Canada? Chicken and egg questions remain exceedingly difficult. Moreover, the moral calculus for judging such questions is complicated. Christian observers must regret the decline of church practice and Christian belief in Canada, but some American believers may continue to think that important aspects of the recently de-christianized Canadian society— including, for example, violence, peacemaking, and attention to those least able to care for themselves—remain substantially more Christian than comparable aspects of American society. Whatever moral judgment can be made, trying to understand how Canada's exchange of traditional

Christian anchorage for an alternative compass of ideological multiculturalism relates to developments inside the churches as well as shifting cultural tectonics in the broader society remains a considerable puzzle for historical analysis.

On this question, the British sociologist David Martin has recently offered a helpful insight in what amounts to a late postscript to his 1978 book, *A General Theory of Secularization.*[71] That volume argued persuasively that when de-christianization has occurred in modern western nations, it usually takes the pattern of earlier christianization in the same countries. Thus, Russia's top-down, czarist, state-sponsored, monopolistic Eastern Orthodoxy gave way to a top-down, Marxist, state-sponsored, monopolistic atheism. By contrast, in the United States, a democratic and voluntaristic Christian society in which churches competed vigorously with each other has been replaced by a pluralistic and voluntaristic democracy in which religious bodies still compete with each other but also with all sorts of other organizations, including government—and on roughly equal footing. In a recent essay specifically on Canada, Martin explains the situation in Quebec by comparison with other nations where Catholics had also enjoyed a territorial base in a largely Protestant society and notes how rapidly such a Catholicism has given way when it secures a "parity of esteem" with the surrounding Protestant culture. Similarly, he shows how developments among Canadian Protestants parallel similar developments in Australia where "the

---

[71] David Martin, *A General Theory of Secularization* (New York: Harper & Row, 1978).

latent power built up by evangelical fervor was now being expended without renewal so that conversion was translated in decency." In Martin's view, this Protestant situation embodies a neat historical symmetry: "The churches that helped form the image of a caring service for others and of mutual help were themselves reformed in the image of what they created."[72]

To extend this interpretation, it was critical that Canada's most important churches themselves advocated, promoted, and facilitated rupture with hereditary patterns of Canadian religious life. They did so, moreover, in circumstances where political contention and economic modernization were creating breaks with a whole range of traditional social practices. Canadian churches, with their heritage of orderly, measured, communal denominational life, were not nearly as well prepared for adjusting to such rapid ruptures as were the more entrepreneurial denominations, interest groups, and para-church agencies of the United States.

Yet if rupture with the past was uppermost in Canadian consciousness, the shape of that consciousness remained more communal and more uniform than in the United States. New public values replaced influences that the Canadian churches had exerted from the eighteenth century through the mid-twentieth. Liberal-communal political ideals stimulated by the Charter of Rights and Freedoms replaced the conservative-communal ideals of Canada's past. Because Christianity had been expressed consistently

---

[72] David Martin, "Canada in Comparative Perspective," in *Rethinking Church, State, and Modernity*, 24, 31, 32.

in the ideals of a conservative-communal social order, when that conservative-communal social order was given up, so also was the Christianity. Rupture with the past, however, did not mean abandonment of a relatively more communal social order as such; it has meant, rather, abandonment of the Christian presence that did so much to build that social order and also provided so much of its substance. In the United States, secularization has proceeded *alongside of* the fragmented, populist structures of American churches. In Canada, by contrast, it has *worked through* the communal, top-down structures of traditional Canadian society.

David Martin's recent extension of his thesis on modern Western secularization advances slightly beyond his earlier work by introducing an explicitly spiritual note. Martin now suggests that "we need to integrate our sociology, and our social history of institutions with what people feel able to say about God and Jesus and what selected aspects of the Christian gospel they feel able to preach." According to Martin, full analysis of why Christian cultures de-christianize needs "to integrate the kind of social history dealing with the local evolution of religious institutions with the content of Christian messages and especially teachings about God and redemption. The decline of preaching presumably has something to do with a diminishing stock of things to say."[73] In my view, Martin is correct that, while social analysis of large-scale forces over time and historical interpretation of key events and personalities can be most

---

[73] Ibid., 33.

illuminating, such analyses, when applied to the Christian churches, require Christian understanding as well.

It is possible to go even further than Martin and say that a providential mystery undergirds all great changes in the earthly fortunes of all Christian churches. Believers in the Incarnation can expect spiritual causality to run concurrently alongside this-worldly causality. Nonetheless, whatever may be concluded about such spiritual realities, attention to the worldly factors canvassed in this study provides at least some hints to explain a considerable puzzle—how Canada, which for so long looked much more Christian than Western Europe, and considerably more Christian than its southern neighbor, now appears in its religious character to resemble Europe much more closely than it does the United States.

CPSIA information can be obtained at www.ICGtesting.com
Printed in the USA
LVOW13s2255230514

387190LV00001B/183/A